Dedication

I dedicate this book, *Facing Up to Failure*, to my four wonderful children, Ben, Ryan, Rachel, and AJ. As you grow into maturity you will come to learn that there are two spiritual forces in this world, the force of darkness and the force of light.

The force of light is the living God. He is ever present to help you achieve your greatest expectations. The force of darkness is the devil. He will attempt to steal your greatest expectations with whatever is available to him.

But if you will place your faith in God, face up to your own shortcomings, allow Him by His Spirit to strengthen you in your inner man, and turn a deaf ear to idle gossip, you will grow to be "world-shakers" for Him.

Contents

Acknowledgments

I would like to thank my wife, Gerri, the staff at Reach Out For Christ–Hyde Park, and our friend, Renee Bolos, for their dedicated assistance in making it possible for the publication of my first three books.

Foreword

I believe this book, *Facing Up to Failure,* is a book that has been crying out to be put into print for many years.

Everyone who reads this book will see that Dr. Wayne Gwilliam has been anointed by the Holy Spirit to put into words and on paper those things which we might have been thinking. And yet, these truths have never been preached in many circles.

Failure seems to always be swept under the table or into the closet — hidden away so that it is not seen and not dealt with. How many of God's chosen are sitting by the "highway of life" not achieving God's best for their lives because of a failure or set back that they allowed to sideline them from the game of life?

Great achievers in the world of business or sport have had one major characteristic — the ability to bounce back to victory after the worst possible failures. Without great battles there can never be great victories!

Echoing in our minds constantly should be the apostle Paul's words, "Forgetting the past, I press toward the mark for the prize of the high calling of God in Jesus Christ. Let us lay aside every weight, and the sin which does so easily beset us, and let us run with patience the race that is set before us. Looking unto Jesus the author and finisher of our faith!" We are not running the hundred yard dash — but a cross country!

Therefore, with great joy I recommend this book to you. Allow God to speak to you and release you into a freedom that you have never experienced.

I count it a privilege to have Dr. Wayne Gwilliam as a friend and close associate and appreciate the anointing on his life and family and ministry. He has a great understanding of love, forgiveness, and acceptance. He not only preaches this, but I have personally witnessed him putting into practice the very truths he has shared in this book.

I believe the Holy Spirit has raised up Dr. Gwilliam as a voice for the 90's, and I am confident that many of God's servants and saints will be set free as they read this remarkable book, *Facing Up to Failure*.

Dr. Rodney Howard-Browne
R.H.B.E.A.
Louisville, Kentucky, U.S.A.

Introduction

For some time I have felt prompted in my spirit to write this book on the subject of facing up to failure. I pray that the Holy Spirit will use it as an instrument of revelation for many brethren to pry free their guilt-ridden minds from the personal shortcomings they have experienced in their lives, thereby causing them to face up to these failures so they may continue to run with diligence toward the vision that God has called them to.

My motivation in revealing the temporary setbacks of any notable person's life, living or dead, is not to impress the reader by my knowledge in this area, nor is it to expose or condemn any of these great men and women. We must never forget the great part they have played in our Christian heritage.

My motivation is strictly to impress upon the readers that they themselves are not the author of failure and that they are not the only ones to have fallen short of God's best for their Christian life; also, just like the great men and women before them, they also can pick up the broken pieces of their lives and continue to press forward toward the mark of their high calling in Jesus Christ.

Guidance for the Wounded Believer

Many books have been written giving testimony to the saving grace of the Lord Jesus Christ that will deliver the reader out of the kingdom of darkness and into the kingdom of light. However, very few books have been written that will give guidance to the believer who — has stumbled in his or her Christian walk. As a matter of fact, to the best of my knowledge, most Christian literature available today would deter any sincere believer from exposing any weakness, past or present, he or she may have.

I have found that the majority of the Church live in the fear of the rejection and the reproach that they have witnessed others receive from the Body of Christ after confessing a problem in their lives, while seeking restoration.

Shoot the Rabbit!

A good illustration that bears testimony to this sad truth is an account I once read of an elderly evangelist giving counsel to a young upcoming ministry on how to bring his shortcomings into the light.

The older man, speaking from his life's experience, informed the young man, "Son, if you have anything in the closet of your life to confess, go for a drive into the desert, find a jack rabbit and confess your sin to it. Then, after you have, shoot the jack rabbit!"

It's a shame for a person to view the Body of Christ in this manner, let alone record it as a tool of instruction for the Body, especially in the light of such Scripture verses as James 5:16a, "Confess your faults one to another, and pray one for another, that you may be healed." Proverbs 28:13 instructs, "He that covereth his sins shall not prosper: but whoso confesseth and forsaketh them shall have mercy."

Confession of Failures

This truth should not be taken to an extreme — either by creating the confessional booth, as some church denominations have, or practicing the cloak of secrecy to the point of believing that the only person to whom sin should be confessed to is the Lord Jesus Himself.

There is a great portion of truth in both of these view points. The key we should be seeking, however, is balance between the two truths — always remembering that any truth taken to extreme becomes error.

Jesus With Skin On!

I once heard an illustration which seems appropriate in describing the balance the Lord desires His Church to attain. A mother awakened by her child's crying one night, went to the child's bedroom, and asked, "What is wrong?" The child sobbed, "I'm scared." The mother assured her, "You have nothing to be scared about. Jesus is with you." The child answered, "I know, Mommy, but I need Jesus with skin on!"

Friends, there will be times in our lives when the magnitude of a problem or failure becomes so overwhelming that the reality of Jesus being ever with us will seem unrealistic. This is when we need Jesus with skin on! This is when we need someone to confess our situation to; someone who, through the love of Jesus, will cover rather than expose the sin.

I pray this book, *Facing Up to Failure*, will serve a two-fold purpose. Firstly, that any minister of the gospel who reads it will be reminded of the need for integrity in the ministry. Secondly, that any person who has suffered hurt by being exposed unnecessarily by a ministry may find it in their heart to forgive, and will do as I did: seek out a true man of God, be straight with him, then allow the anointing that God has placed on his life to heal your wounded spirit.

—*Wayne Gwilliam*

Chapter 1
The Need for Integrity

At one time or another, we have all witnessed the tragic outcome when a believer, simply wanting to deal with a problem area in his life, experiences one of the most painful events he will ever encounter. The setting for this traumatic occurrence has many times been a local church.

A guilt-filled believer hears the preacher minister on the subject of getting yourself right with God. Being convicted by the message, he confesses his sin to the man who has just preached this wonderful message of restoration. The trusting Christian is then exposed and condemned publicly by the very minister he felt could understand and help him.

The Spiritually Wounded

Friends, the immaturity of these ministers has caused more death and mutilation in the Body of Jesus Christ than can ever be assessed. Literally tens of thousands of wounded Chris-

5

tians will never step foot back into another church, all because of the immaturity of people who have the audacity to call themselves pastors. It is obvious they have never taken to heart Ezekiel 34, where the Lord gives a solemn, prophetic warning to those who would take the responsibility for shepherding His flock.

So often we hear preachers make the statement that the the Church is the only army that shoots its wounded. Sadly, the person who makes this statement needs to heed his own words. I have met this type of ministry all over the world.

One incident that readily comes to mind happened to me in the State of New York, where I had been ministering for several years as an evangelist. I first met this brother at a men's retreat, and he asked me to come and preach for him with the intention of holding a tent crusade in the summer months.

Before the meeting, I was invited to his office for coffee and fellowship, only to have him bend my ear with his disgruntled opinions concerning the other ministers in the city who were experiencing more success in ministry than he was.

His conversation then progressed from the local ministers to his own church members. At this point I realized I was in terrible trouble. The revelation hit me that if I did not perform to a standard satisfactory to him, it would be my ministry that would be his next excuse for failure.

As I suspected, I did not meet his standard, and not a great deal of time passed before his idle chatter filtered back to me. The offense he developed toward me, because I would not return his phone calls in reference to having a tent crusade, only increased as time progressed.

The reason why I did not return his calls was because I did not want to be responsible for sending vulnerable new converts into his church to become the personal slaves of this man and his family! And no doubt they would be further brutalized by this man when they left his church for greener pastures rather than become a part of his little empire.

We have all witnessed what happens to Christians who eventually become fed up with this type of church leadership and seek to find a church where they can grow under the spirit of love, forgiveness, and acceptance. They are branded as rebellious and become marked for life.

A Wounded Spirit Who Can Bear?

The Holy Spirit has done everything possible to warn of the damage that can be caused by this type of recklessness in the ministry. Proverbs 18:8 warns of the hurt that can be caused by loose lips in the Body of Christ. Here Solomon says, "The words of a talebearer are as wounds, and they go down into the innermost parts of the belly."

Friends, I believe when we become a tale-bearer we truly take upon ourselves the character of the demonic realm. The name "talebearer" originated from Satan walking to and fro upon the earth and reporting back to God the short-comings of His people. A picture of a demon or the devil is portrayed with a tail, as an emblem to his character as a talebearer. The New Testament actually calls him "the accuser of the brethren."

Solomon, in his wisdom, warns of the out-working in a person's life once his spirit has been wounded by the betrayal of a friend. He writes in Proverbs 18:14, "The spirit of a man will sustain his infirmity; but a wounded spirit who can bear?"

Possession, or Rejection?

Brethren, when a man's spirit is healthy, it will produce an inner strength to the soul that will enable the person to overcome any sickness or disease. Although a person may suffer the loss of an eye or a limb he could rise above it. The devil knows, however, that once the man's spirit becomes wounded, the man becomes as vulnerable as Samson was after his hair was cut. The end result is a death-wish, to go home to be with the Lord.

I witnessed this truth some years ago in a meeting where several deliverance ministries were trying to cast a spirit of self-destruction out of a woman which they believed entered her through a broken relationship. They had her reeling all over the church floor, coughing and screaming for about an hour.

The Holy Spirit instructed me to tell them it was not a demon, but rather her own spirit that had been wounded and no longer wanted to stay in the woman's body. Her wounded spirit consequently drove her to try to take her life.

The Lord then gave me several words of knowledge about the woman's situation that opened her up to the anointing. At that very *true* moment she broke down and wept uncontrollably as the sting of the betrayal filtered out through her soul. This woman has been able to cope with her situation ever since.

A Faithful Spirit Conceals a Matter

Friends, I have been with preachers, and have been one myself, who have taken lightly the sincere confessions of vulnerable believers who have shared the shortfalls of their lives in response to the message of repentance preached. The believer then leaves the meeting believing that everything will be all right, only to discover a week or so later that their confession has been shared carelessly with others.

The betrayal inflicted by the immaturity of the entrusted ministry has now produced more hurt than the unconfessed sin could have caused. Prior to their attempt toward restoration, they were already in poor spiritual condition. Now they find themselves in an even worsened state.

Friends, it is a terrible shame that people who have experienced the integrity of Jesus in concealing their own misfortunes, find it so difficult to express just a portion of that same integrity toward their brethren who have confessed to a questionable act — especially in light of Proverbs 11:13, "A talebearer revealeth secrets: but he that is of a faithful spirit concealeth the matter."

Galatians 6:1,2 gives clear instructions for the Church if a man is overtaken in a fault, "Ye which are spiritual, restore such an one in the spirit of meekness; considering thyself, lest thou also be tempted. Bear ye one another's burdens, and so fulfill the law of Christ."

Message of Love, Forgiveness, Acceptance

It is a tragedy that so many New Testament ministers, commissioned by Christ to preach His message of love, forgiveness, and acceptance, still use the letter of the law to stone to death the spiritually wounded. These ministers should instead become the surgeons Christ purposed for them to be by using as a scalpel the message of grace and mercy, purchased by His own blood, to bring healing to the battered souls of mankind.

Let me use a parable as an illustration. A young girl, still bound by the world system, is seduced by a smooth-talking young man who promises her the moon so he can have his way with her. She then becomes pregnant, and in her distress comes to the church for help.

The church body, desirous to help, extends a compassionate hand toward her. Each member helps the girl and assures her that forgiveness and restoration are available for her in the cross.

Then, not long afterwards, one of the same Christian women who helped this poor young girl experiences a similar situation. She is now scorned by the same church that showed such great mercy to the girl from the world. The shame and hurt from the rejection of her brethren will eventually drive her out into the world system, suffering from the deception that she has committed the unforgivable sin.

The illustration I have just given has been a reality for thousands of young women throughout Christendom. As a matter of fact, Jesus witnessed an example of it while He was preaching on the Mount of Olives. The gospel of John 8:3-10 records, "And the scribes and Pharisees brought unto him a woman taken in adultery; and when they had set her in the midst, They say unto him, Master, this woman was taken in adultery, in the very act. Now Moses in the law commanded us, that such should be stoned: but what sayest thou? This they said, tempting him, that they might have to accuse him. But Jesus stooped down, and with his finger wrote on the ground, as though he heard them not. So when they continued asking him, he lifted up himself, and said unto them, He that is without sin among you, let him first cast a stone at her. And again he stooped down, and wrote on the ground. And they which heard it, being convicted by their own conscience, went out one by one, beginning at the eldest, even unto the last: and Jesus was left alone, and the woman standing in the midst. When Jesus had lifted up himself, and saw none but the woman, he said unto her, Woman, where are those thine accusers? hath no man condemned thee? She said, No man, Lord. And Jesus said unto her, Neither do I condemn thee: go, and sin no more."

Jesus — Our Defense Attorney

The account of this woman caught in adultery is the first place in Scripture where the accused had a defense attorney: Jesus Himself! All too often we confuse our ministerial responsibilities with the responsibilities of the prophets and lawyers who served under the Old Covenant.

You see, the lawyers of the Old Covenant were appointed, under the law, to catch and expose a person in their sin. After the person was exposed, they were then severely punished to the fullest extent of the law. Jesus, in this historic event, portrays the manner in which a minister of the New Covenant should deal with the knowledge of a person's sin.

Notice the hidden gem of truth in this account of the woman taken in adultery: Even though the scribes and pharisees, because of the sin in their own lives, could not stone her, Jesus Himself was compelled, under the law, to stone her because He was without sin! Yet instead of stoning her, He simply said, "Neither do I condemn thee: go and sin no more."

What is Mercy?

The reason the event of the woman caught in adultery is recorded in Scripture is for our instruction. We cannot display mercy until we know for certain that the person is actually guilty and that within the law is subject to punishment. At this point, and only at this point, can we make the decision to show mercy. After all, this is actually what mercy is, is it not?

The priest or prophet of the Old Covenant, however, did not have the authority to administer mercy in this situation. They were covenant-bound to obey the law and administer judgment. Likewise, we also would have been obligated to obey the law and administer judgment, if it were not for the fact that Jesus paid the ransom that was required for this woman's sin. It is the ransom of the blood of Jesus, and this ransom alone, that grants us the right to display true mercy!

Freely Forgive!

But so many New Testament believers can be likened to the person Jesus talked about who owed a king millions of dollars and had no way to pay his debt. So the king forgave him his debt. Not long afterward, this man, who was forgiven so much, crossed paths with a person who owed him only a few dollars and demanded that he pay him the full amount or suffer the full consequences of the law.

This event is recorded in the gospel of Matthew 18:23-35, "Therefore is the kingdom of heaven likened unto a certain king, which would take account of his servants. And when he had begun to reckon, one was brought unto him, which owed him ten thousand talents. But forasmuch as he had not to pay, his lord commanded him to be sold, and his wife, and children, and all that he had, and payment to be made. The servant therefore fell down, and worshipped him, saying, Lord, have patience with me, and I will pay thee all. Then the lord of that servant was moved with compassion, and loosed him, and forgave him the debt. But the same servant went out, and found one of his fellowservants, which owed him an hundred pence: and he laid hands on him, and took him by the throat, saying, Pay me that thou owest. And his fellowservant fell down at his feet, and besought him, saying, Have patience with me, and I will pay thee all. And he would not: but went and cast him into prison, till he should pay the debt. So when his fellowservants saw what was done, they were very sorry, and came and told unto their lord all that was done. Then his lord, after that he had called him, said unto him, O thou wicked servant, I forgave thee all that debt, because thou desiredst me: Shouldest not thou also have had compassion on thy fellowservant, even as I had pity on thee? And his lord was wroth, and delivered him to the tormentors, till he should pay all that was due unto him. So likewise shall my heavenly Father do also unto you, if ye from your hearts forgive not every one his brother their trespasses."

Message for the Church — Restore!

If ever there is a prophetic message for the Church today, given by one of the prophets of old, it would certainly have to be Isaiah 42:18-23, where Isaiah says, "Hear, ye deaf; and look, ye blind, that ye may see. Who is blind, but my servant? or deaf, as my messenger that I sent? who is blind as he that is perfect, and blind as the Lord's servant? Seeing many things, but thou observest not; opening the ears, but he heareth not. The Lord is well pleased for his righteousness' sake; he will magnify the law, and make it honourable. But this is a people robbed and spoiled; they are all of them snared in holes, and they are hid in prison houses: they are for a prey, and none delivereth; for a spoil, and none saith, Restore. Who among you will give ear to this? who will hearken and hear for the time to come?"

Brethren, the Church will never see the harvest of souls we have been desperately waiting for until the apostle Paul's prayer for the Ephesian church is fully comprehended. Paul prayed that these believers would receive the revelation of Christ's love that passes knowledge, that they might be filled with all the fullness of God.

It is time our emotions are brought into check! No longer should the Church be governed by the knowledge of a person's sin, but rather be governed by the total forgiveness that was granted to all mankind on the cross of Calvary.

Chapter 2

Love That Heals

The Lord Jesus Christ began His ministry with a proclamation from the book of Isaiah 61:1-2 as recorded in Luke 4:18,19. He said, "The Spirit of the Lord is upon me, because he hath anointed me to preach the gospel to the poor; he hath sent me to heal the brokenhearted, to preach deliverance to the captives, and recovering of sight to the blind, to set at liberty them that are bruised. To preach the acceptable year of the Lord."

Christ has commissioned His Church to carry out this same proclamation that He so boldly made in the Temple nearly 2000 years ago. The very reason the Holy Spirit was poured out upon the 120 disciples on the Day of Pentecost, was to enable the Church to heal the broken hearted and set at liberty them that are bruised. Christ has not sent us into this world to condemn it, but rather to proclaim salvation and healing to it!

Healing Message to the Church

Tragically, the hurt that Jesus commissioned His Church to heal has just not affected those under the control of the world system. But many Christians, too, have fallen prey to the devil's evil schemes. The Church has become a battlefield, littered with countless thousands of broken and wounded believers who are also in need of the healing message of Christ.

Many believers have fallen prey to the high expectations of what they personally believe the Lord has called them to, or what others have convinced them they were called to. As a result of failing, they have been wounded and have become lethargic in their Christian witness. Some have even retreated to a place in the wilderness, as Moses did.

Moses fell short of what he believed the Lord required of him as a leader when he killed a man in trying to fulfill his call to the ministry of reconciliation. Just like Moses, many have brought death, rather than life, to those they genuinely loved and sincerely wanted to help.

The weapon of destruction in this instance has not been the fist, but the letter of the law. Then, just as Moses did, they have condemned themselves and run and hid in a wasteland from the real purpose of God for their lives.

However, Moses was not the only person in Scripture to fall short of God's plan for his life.

King David also battled with this problem. He found that Goliath was easier to conquer than his own spirit.

Proverbs 16:32 counsels, "He that is slow to anger is better than the mighty; and he that ruleth his spirit then he that taketh a city." Again in Proverbs 25:28 Solomon declares, "He that hath no rule over his own spirit is like a city that is broken down, and without walls."

I personally believe that Solomon wrote these wise sayings by reflecting with hindsight on his father's life: by viewing all his father's victories in battle over the enemies of Israel, and by acknowledging the defeats his father personally suffered through lack of self-control in the realm of his own spirit.

David Understands God's Mercy

King David suffered his first failure when he desired another man's wife. This great king, in having defeated the champion of the Philistine army, the giant Goliath, and in having won battle after battle, conquering city after city, and even remaining steadfast throughout all of Saul's onslaughts against his life, fell prey to the lust of his own heart.

David's fall had a devastating effect on his life as revealed in Psalm 38:1-12, "O Lord, rebuke me not in thy wrath: neither chasten me in thy hot displeasure. For thine arrows stick fast in me, and thy hand presseth me sore. There is no soundness in my flesh because of thine anger; neither is there any rest in my bones because of my sin. For mine iniquities are gone over mine head: as an heavy burden they are too heavy for me. My wounds stink and are corrupt because of my foolishness. I am troubled; I am bowed down greatly; I go mourning all the day long. For my loins are filled with a loathsome disease: and there is no soundness in my flesh. I am feeble and sore broken: I have roared by reason of the disquietness of my heart. Lord, all my desire is before thee; and my groaning is not hid from thee. My heart panteth, my strength faileth me: as for the light of mine eyes, it also is gone from me. My lovers and my friends stand aloof from my sore; and my kinsmen stand afar off. They also that seek after my life lay snares for me: and they that seek my hurt speak mischievous things, and imagine deceits all the day long."

The Law Was Not a Despot

No doubt David, like Moses before him, had fallen from grace and now was paying the price of sin in his relationship with God. He deserved to lose his kingdom and all his wealth, along with his unquestionable reputation. As a matter of fact, under the laws of Israel, both David and Bathsheba should have been dragged out of the city and stoned. They had not only committed adultery; they had also committed murder.

The very fact that this did not happen is proof that the law was not implemented to be an absolute dictator, but was a schoolmaster to the people of Israel. The Israelites took the law to be absolute. However, God never meant it to be this way at all.

The Lord never killed a person in the Old or New Covenant who gave heed to the message of repentance. Only those who refused to acknowledge and repent of their sins paid the consequences of their sin.

The Great Escape Route!

God is not a tyrant! David, in the midst of his depression, realized the great mercy of God when he remembered the escape route built into the law through the blood sacrifice that was offered for the sins of Israel upon the brazen altar.

The impact this revelation had on David is recorded in Psalm 51. He makes his statement of repentance, saying, "Have mercy upon me, O God, according to thy lovingkindness: according unto the multitude of thy tender mercies blot out my transgressions. Wash me thoroughly from my iniquity, and cleanse me from my sin. For I acknowledge my transgressions: and my sin is ever before me. Against thee, thee only, have I sinned, and done this evil in thy sight:

that thou mightest be justified when thou speakest, and be clear when thou judgest. Behold, I was shapen in iniquity; and in sin did my mother conceive me. Behold, thou desirest truth in the inward parts: and in the hidden part thou shalt make me to know wisdom. Purge me with hyssop, and I shall be clean: wash me, and I shall be whiter than snow."

Friends, all too often in the midst of the guilt and shame of the fall, the cleansing power of the blood of Jesus Christ is forgotten.

This reminds me of a brutal murder that occurred when a woman was confronted in her living room by her attacker.

In the fear of the moment, she escaped to the closet for safety, but forgot a loaded gun had been kept there by her husband. In reality, there was a way out of this impossible situation all the time. If only she had remembered the gun!

David in the midst of his hopeless state remembered that God had made provision within the law for such an occasion as this. In Psalm 32 he expresses his thanks to God for His great mercy.

David says in Psalm 32:1-7, "Blessed is he whose transgression is forgiven, whose sin is covered. Blessed is the man unto whom the Lord imputeth not iniquity, and in whose spirit there is no guile. When I kept silence, my bones waxed old through my roaring all the day long.

For day and night thy hand was heavy upon me: my moisture is turned into the drought of summer. Selah. I acknowledged my sin unto thee, and mine iniquity have I not hid. I said, I will confess my transgressions unto the Lord; and thou forgavest the iniquity of my sin. Selah. For this shall every one that is godly pray unto thee in a time when thou mayest be found: surely in the floods of great waters they shall not come nigh unto him. Thou art my hiding place; thou shalt preserve me from trouble; thou shalt compass me about with the songs of deliverance. Selah."

The Compassion of a Loving Savior

Jonah certainly knew the compassion of God's nature, and for this very reason he did not want to go to Nineveh. The Assyrians were a threat to the known world at that time. Their cruelty against their neighboring nations was legendary. Jonah, who had witnessed their violent acts against mankind, wanted God to utterly destroy the Assyrian people. Jonah did not want to go to preach the message of repentance. He knew that if the Assyrians acted upon God's warning to them, the Lord, being full of compassion, would forgive them. And this is exactly what happened! Jonah was angry!

In the book of Jonah 4:4-11 (NKJV) the Lord confronts Jonah about his attitude, "Then the Lord said, 'Is it right for you to be angry?' So

Jonah went out of the city and sat on the east side of the city. There he made himself a shelter and sat under it in the shade, till he might see what would become of the city. And the Lord God prepared a plant and made it come up over Jonah, that it might be shade for his head to deliver him from his misery. So Jonah was very grateful for the plant. But as morning dawned the next day God prepared a worm, and it so damaged the plant that it withered. And it happened, when the sun arose, that God prepared a vehement east wind; and the sun beat on Jonah's head, so that he grew faint. Then he wished death for himself, and said, 'It is better for me to die than to live.' Then God said to Jonah, 'Is it right for you to be angry about the plant?' And he said, 'It is right for me to be angry, even to death!' But the Lord said, 'You have had pity on the plant for which you have not labored, nor made it grow, which came up in a night and perished in a night. And should I not pity Nineveh, that great city, in which are more than one hundred and twenty thousand persons who cannot discern between their right hand and their left, and also much livestock?'"

Sadly, there are many "Jonahs" in the Body of Christ who would prefer to see the Lord destroy the wicked rather than restore them.

I have been guilty of this terrible sin myself. I have also witnessed it in the lives of many preachers in churches and on street corners around the world. They proclaim the message of judgment and destruction with vengeance in their voices, rather than voicing the compassion of a loving Savior, compelling the lost to come home. In many cases, it is not even what they are saying; it is the way they are saying it!

An Illustration of the Father's Love

There is a tremendous illustration of the love of the Father found in Luke's gospel, chapter 15:11-32, where Jesus said, "A certain man had two sons: And the younger of them said to his father, Father, give me the portion of goods that falleth to me. And he divided unto them his living. And not many days after the younger son gathered all together, and took his journey into a far country, and there wasted his substance with riotous living. And when he had spent all, there arose a mighty famine in that land: and he began to be in want. And he went and joined himself to a citizen of that country; and he sent him into his fields to feed swine. And he would fain have filled his belly with the husks that the swine did eat: and no man gave unto him. And when he came to himself, he said, How many hired servants of my father's have bread enough and to spare, and I perish with hunger! I will arise and go to my father, and will say unto him, Father, I have sinned against heaven, and before thee, And am no more worthy to be called thy son: make me as one of thy hired servants. And he arose, and came to his father. But when he was yet a great way off, his father saw him, and had compassion, and ran, and fell on his neck, and kissed him. And the son said unto him, Father, I have sinned against heaven, and in thy sight, and am no more worthy to be called thy son. But the father said to his servants, Bring forth the best robe, and put it on him; and put a ring on his hand, and shoes on his feet: And bring hither the fatted calf, and kill it; and let us eat, and be merry: For this my son was dead, and is alive again; he was lost, and is found. And they began to be merry. Now his elder son was in the field: and as he came and drew nigh to the house, he heard music and dancing. And he called one of the servants, and asked what these things meant. And he said unto him, Thy brother is come; and thy father hath killed the fatted calf, because he hath received him safe and sound. And he was angry, and would not go in: therefore came his father out, and intreated him. And he answering said to his father, Lo, these many years do I serve thee, neither transgressed I at any time thy commandment: and yet thou never gavest me a kid, that I might make merry with my friends: But as soon as this thy son was come, which hath devoured thy living with harlots, thou hast killed for him the fatted calf. And he said unto him, Son, thou art ever with me, and all that I have is thine. It was meet that we should make merry, and be glad: for this thy brother was dead, and is alive again; and was lost, and is found."

Know Your Father's Heart

Many sermons have been preached on this famous text of Scripture, ranging from the maturity of the father and the immaturity of the younger son, to the stubbornness of the older brother. I would like to bring your attention to the inability of both sons to understand the forgiving heart of their father.

The younger son actually expected the father to punish him by accepting him as a second rate person, or a servant. In the deepest recesses of his mind, he did not expect to receive the mercy that was extended to him.

The older brother, who witnessed the mercy of the father toward his wayward younger brother, became very angry that his father could even think of showing such "sloppy agape" to this inconsiderate, lowdown, good-for-nothing, poor-excuse-for-a-son who had squandered all his money on reckless living.

Thank God that the father, and not the older brother, saw the younger son coming home. Can you imagine in your mind's eye the conversation the older brother would have had with the younger brother? Believe me I can!

I have heard this conversation a thousand times in churches, Bible schools, and on church boards around the world. I have heard the religious older brother speak to the backslidden younger brother. I can tell you what I have heard has not been the same love, forgiveness, and acceptance that the father demonstrated toward the wayward son.

I have even heard one renowned preacher teach, facetiously, that he overheard the father speaking to his eldest son, assuring him that all his younger brother would ever get is the new suit and shoes, the ring, and the party, and that everything else belonged to him.

Well, I have news for that preacher, and it's all bad! The Father never rejected Moses or David. Jesus never rejected the prostitute or anyone else who came to Him. As a matter of fact, He still accepted Peter, even after Peter had denied Him three times.

We don't know whether the older brother, like the younger, saw the need to receive the forgiveness demonstrated in the heart of the father for his selfish attitude toward his younger brother. I pray he did!

Chapter 3
Understanding Failure

Webster's dictionary defines "failure" as "One who or that which fails. A proving unsuccessful in business or other ventures, by neglect or non-performance of a duty."

Failure is as old as man. The first man to fail was the first man, Adam, when he disobeyed God in the Garden of Eden. The next was Cain when he killed his brother, Abel. Jacob also failed God when he deceived his father to receive his brother's blessing. Noah failed God when he got drunk. Moses failed God when he killed a man.

Lot failed God when he slept with his daughters. Abraham failed God when he took Hagar as his mistress. Samson failed God when he slept around and cut his hair. David failed God when he took another man's wife and then had the husband killed.

Eli failed God when he failed to discipline his children. Samuel failed God when he appointed his children as judges over Israel knowing that they did not walk in the ways of God. Jonah failed God when he ran away from his commission. Gideon failed God when he took the spoil of the Midianites for himself instead of sharing it with the entire army.

Failure is Not Terminal

Friends, failure was a common occurrence in the lives of the great men and women of the Bible. It is definitely not something new to God. But sadly, when faced with failure, we feel we are the only person in the world to have ever failed God. Frankly, it is intensified more in our minds than it is in anyone else's mind.

Like all those who have failed before us, we have to identify failure and face up to it, realizing that it does not have to be terminal and can be dealt with easily once you have discovered the root of its existence in your life.

A Testimony

My greatest failure happened when I pastored a church in Australia, in a country town of some thirty thousand people. This church was my first real pastorate, and I was eager to prove myself to my peers as well as to seek God's approval.

When I took the church over as pastor, there were about thirty people in the congregation. I was a young, thirty-year-old preacher with "forty years experience," and within the first three years of becoming pastor, the church grew to nearly two hundred people. In the Australian state where the church was located, this growth was considered to be extraordinary.

During this same period, we had also completed extensive renovations on the old church building. Up until this point I personally believed that I was doing a good job as pastor, and I am sure that my congregation and the denomination I was credentialed with believed this also.

Then one Sunday morning a dear sister who had been in the church for some years prophesied that it was time to enlarge the borders of our tent, and if we would be obedient to fulfill this prophecy, God would give us the city.

Even though no one in the congregation had any experience in building such an extensive complex, we accepted the challenge and became quite intoxicated with the fact that God had chosen this body of believers to be the vessel to reach the city and to build a place of worship for Him.

So we scouted the city to find the right block of land to build our new worship center. When we found it, we put the old church up for sale, and within a short time found a buyer. With the monies we received from the sale, we purchased the property for our new worship center.

The next step was to have blueprints drawn up and secure the money so that we could begin to build. A friend in the church agreed to loan the church seventy thousand dollars, and the bank agreed to lend another one hundred and fifty thousand, making a total of two hundred and twenty thousand dollars — not a lot of money to erect a double brick structure that consisted of a six-hundred seat auditorium, a Bible school to seat one hundred students, an administration area with six executive offices, and a kitchen equipped to cater for six hundred people.

We also had to bring in heavy earthmoving equipment to build a road and prepare the foundation site for the main building. We had to hire a large bulldozer, a grader, a backhoe, a large vibrator roller, two dump trucks and drivers to work twelve hours a day for two weeks carrying gravel for the necessary preparation of the foundation for the main building.

We also had to complete major renovations on the three-bedroom house already on the property. To top all that off, we purchased two more buildings from the local hospital, moved them onto the property, believing we would save money, only to discover that after we had finished renovating, they actually cost more to restore than to build.

Then we had to buy the rug for the floor, six hundred chairs for the auditorium, one hundred seats for the Bible school, a sound system, a grand piano, office furniture, a photo copier to handle the combined work load of the church, the Bible school, and the primary school, furniture to equip the primary school, a telephone system to handle the work load of the church, a water reservoir and pumping system, and a septic system to handle the complex.

The town then charged me to upgrade the electrical transformer. In addition, there was the landscaping and many other hidden costs too numerous to mention.

As you can imagine, we went over budget. Although the congregation was growing rapidly, our converts were problem people and most were unemployed. Many drug addicts and troubled youth found their way to our church from all over the nation. This influx produced new problems within the church.

We bought more land and buildings to develop a rehabilitation center, and this property needed restoration. This all happened in just over eighteen months, and we now owed around three hundred thousand dollars — very little for what we had accomplished! But even though our congregation had grown and our needs had become greater, the offerings remained basically the same.

The financial pressure forced me to spend more time out on the road to raise the necessary finances to keep the church afloat. Eventually, I was totally burned out, so I handed the church over to another pastor. But I was now left with a sense of failure in my life which would take the next three years to recover from completely.

Friends, there was nothing wrong with my desire to do something great for God, and there was nothing wrong with the vision of the church desiring to minister to those oppressed and in need. I truly believe that God had spoken to me just as He had spoken to Moses. But like Moses, I let my ambitions get confused with my capability.

Exercising Leadership

Moses discerned the will of God for his life by the supernatural desire that burned within him to set the oppressed free. Then he tried to fulfill his desire in the flesh. This brought death, rather than life, to the people Moses was sent to minister to.

Like Moses, I had to come to the conclusion that this failure was in me, not in God or the people. Often we try to pass the buck and make excuses — if only God would have done this, or if the people would have done that, the end result would have been different.

But God invests the responsibility of the leadership of His people into hands of His five-fold ministry! A leader only becomes a leader in the midst of controversy. Frankly, any fool can lead when everything is going well!

Why Criest Unto Me!

Moses learned this principle of leadership when he was confronted by an impossible situation at the Red Sea. To the front of him was the sea, and behind him was Pharaoh and his army. There was no place to run! He quickly tried to relinquish his leadership back to God.

The account of this event is found in Exodus 14:13-16, "And Moses said unto the people, Fear ye not, stand still, and see the salvation of the Lord, which he will shew to you to day: for the Egyptians whom ye have seen today, ye shall see them again no more for ever. The Lord shall fight for you, and ye shall hold your peace. And the Lord said unto Moses, Wherefore criest thou unto me? speak unto the children of Israel, that they go forward: But lift thou up thy rod, and stretch out thine hand over the sea, and divide it: and the children of Israel shall go on dry ground through the midst of the sea."

From studying these verses of Scripture, it is obvious that Moses was intimidated by the magnitude of the problem he was facing. In his dilemma, he tried to give the responsibility of leadership back to God. Surprisingly, Moses discovered that God would not take it back. The Lord told Moses to lead the people on and to divide the sea by using the rod, or the resource of power that was contained within the gift that He had entrusted to Moses' keeping.

This great historic account gives clarity to the Scripture found in Proverbs 18:16, "A man's gift maketh room for him, and bringeth him before great men."

Identifying Failure

Friends, to be able to successfully deal with failure we must learn to identify failure. The seeds of failure are in us — not in God or in those whom we would blame for the failure. I, like thousands of others before me, had to come to this conclusion, even though I could have dumped my guilt into a multitude of places that seemed quite genuine.

The Lord eventually made me face up to the inadequacy in my own soul, produced from the sense of failure I had experienced when I pastored that country church in Australia.

Early in 1991, He brought me into a worse situation than the church I left in Australia. He asked me to take the reins of a church that had bought a twenty-nine acre property and built a 900-seat auditorium, Bible school and caretaker's house, and had a debt and deficit larger than my previous church.

The church had just suffered a split, leaving it with thirty-five committed adults and a weekly income of two thousand dollars. Because of my previous failure, I felt like running away from what God had asked me to do. It was only the assurance that He produced in my spirit by consistently reassuring me that He was the great I AM — just as He had done for Moses — that propelled me beyond what seemed would be my greatest defeat yet.

But thank God for the years I spent soul searching and rehashing every decision that I ever made while I pastored that church in Australia. This gave me the insight and courage to take on this impossible task and to see God's deliverance in my life and the life of this church.

In just one year, the debts have been caught up, the building completed, and the membership is approximately six hundred people.

Chapter 4

Developing Your Capabilities

Many Christians truly believe that God will reward them for effort rather than production. Let's go to Scripture to discredit this fable.

In Matthew 25:14-30, Christ gives the basic blueprint for empowering and accountability for that which has been entrusted to the believer.

Jesus explains, "For the kingdom of heaven is as a man traveling into a far country, who called his own servants, and delivered unto them his goods. And unto one he gave five talents, to another two, and to another one; to every man according to his several ability; and straightway took his journey. Then he that had received the five talents went and traded with the same, and made them other five talents. And likewise he that had received two, he also gained other two. But he that had received one went and digged in the earth, and hid his lord's money. After a long time the lord of those servants cometh, and reckoneth with them. And

39

so he that had received five talents came and brought other five talents, saying, Lord, thou deliveredst unto me five talents: behold, I have gained beside them five talents more. His lord said unto him, Well done, thou good and faithful servant: thou hast been faithful over a few things, I will make thee ruler over many things: enter thou into the joy of thy lord. He also that had received two talents came and said, Lord, thou deliveredst unto me two talents: behold, I have gained two other talents beside them. His lord said unto him, Well done, good and faithful servant; thou hast been faithful over a few things, I will make thee ruler over many things: enter thou into the joy of thy lord. Then he which had received the one talent came and said, Lord, I knew thee that thou art an hard man, reaping where thou hast not sown, and gathering where thou hast not strawed: And I was afraid, and went and hid thy talent in the earth: lo, there thou hast that is thine. His lord answered and said unto him, Thou wicked and slothful servant, thou knewest that I reap where I sowed not, and gather where I have not strawed: Thou oughtest therefore to have put my money to the exchangers, and then at my coming I should have received mine own with usury. Take therefore the talent from him, and give it unto him which have ten talents. For unto every one that hath shall be given, and he shall have abundance: but from him that hath not shall be taken away even that which he hath."

The key to a powerful infilling of the Holy Spirit is found in verse 15, where Jesus instructs that He will neither over-commit nor under-commit us. He gives according to our ability, not according to our desire.

The Lord did not love the man he gave five talents to more than He loved the man He gave two talents to. He did not love the man He gave two talents to more than the man He gave one talent to. He gave to each according to their ability!

Christ Gives According to Our Ability

This simple truth is often overlooked: many Christians, seeking a greater empowering for their ministry, attempt to buy the anointing with their efforts. They spend many hours in prayer and fasting, believing their efforts will afford them a greater anointing.

If only they realized that they are actually using the same tactics used by Simon the sorcerer after witnessing the power of God being demonstrated through the apostles!

The account of Simon the sorcerer found in Acts 8:18-23 says, "And when Simon saw that through laying on of the apostles' hands the Holy Ghost was given, he offered them money, saying, Give me also this power, that on whomsoever I lay hands, he may receive the Holy Ghost. But Peter said unto him, Thy money perish with thee, because thou hast thought that the gift of God may be purchased with money. Thou hast neither part nor lot in this matter: for thy heart is not right in the sight of God. Repent therefore of this thy wickedness, and pray God, if perhaps the thought of thine heart may be forgiven thee. For I perceive that thou art in the gall of bitterness, and in the bond of iniquity."

I have seen many Christians motivated by the same spirit that Simon was driven by. Some go on long fasts and spend many hours in prayer. Others give all their time and money to a local church only to find themselves in massive debt, and then become offended with the ministry of the church because that ministry never placed them in a prominent position.

They then leave the church, slandering the pastor, saying they were used and abused. If only these people would come to the revelation that God does not take bribes.

Discipline Develops Abilities

Brethren, we must understand that our Lord gives according to our abilities! Our abilities do not grow on trees, nor can they be purchased at the local store. Abilities are developed within the soul by the believer being disciplined into his call by the leadership that the Lord has given charge over him.

Hebrews 13 verses 7 and 17 clearly reveals this. In verse 7 we read, "Remember them which have the rule over you, who have spoken unto you the word of God: whose faith follow, considering the end of their conversation."

And in verse 17 we read, "Obey them that have the rule over you, and submit yourselves: for they watch for your souls, as they that must give account, that they may do it with joy, and not with grief: for that is unprofitable for you."

Recognize the Need to Learn

So many believers are under the assumption that if God calls you, He will equip you to do the work of your mission in life, whether it be the five-fold ministry or serving as a deacon, song leader, usher, church secretary, bus driver, husband, wife, or parent.

According to Ephesians 4:11-14, "And he gave some, apostles, prophets; and some, evangelists; and some pastors and teachers; For the perfecting of the saints, for the work of the ministry, for the edifying of the body of Christ. Till we all come into the unity of the faith, and of the knowledge of the Son of God, unto a perfect man, unto the measure of the stature of the fullness of Christ: That we henceforth be no more children, tossed to and fro, and carried about with every wind of doctrine, by the sleight of men, and cunning craftiness, whereby they lie in wait to deceive."

If we were to fully believe that God bestows total maturity on the believer by the infilling of the Holy Ghost, the five-fold ministry would be nothing more than ornaments to dress up the Church. Therefore, Scriptures like the ones we have just read would have to be removed from the Bible.

This type of mentality is one of the main roots from which the tree of failure grows. This root needs to be dealt with so that the full benefit is received from the ministries that have been given to the Church to bring all believers into maturity.

This root of deception within the believer's life is destroyed by recognizing the need to learn. Then he must make the decision to place himself under the leadership of a local church serviced by a continual flow of the five-fold ministry so that a balanced understanding of the gospel is achieved.

So many of the local churches in the world today are controlled by just one ministry — the pastor. This will cause the congregation to grow with an unbalanced view of the gospel.

Inability Within the Soul

When we take the life of King Saul into consideration, the Bible teaches that he was anointed with the Holy Spirit, and at that point he was turned into a different man and won some great victories for the Lord. But because he did not develop self-control within the realm of his emotions and was led astray from the purpose of the Lord by doing that which was right in his own eyes, he lost his right to rule within the kingdom of God.

There is nothing wrong with the vision, the desire, or the anointing on the believer's life. It is the inability within the soul to handle the vision, the anointing, and the desire!

Our Desires vs. God's Desires

You may ask if the ability to handle the desire, the vision, and the anointing is not present, how did you get them in the first place? I am glad you asked that question. Please let me explain by taking you to an event that occurred in Scripture: Israel's request for a king.

There was nothing wrong with this request. I personally believe the desire for a king was established in the hearts of the Israelites by God so He could make way for His chosen king, David, from whose seed Jesus was to come forth.

But, David, God's chosen, was still a "twinkle in his father's eye" when Israel demanded a king. Israel "jumped the gun" and ran before they were sent, and received Saul as king. It was because of their impetuous ways that they put themselves through a lot of unnecessary pain, because they did not allow God to mentally condition and prepare them to bring about His purpose in the fullness of time.

This event is found in First Samuel 8:4-22, "Then all the elders of Israel gathered themselves together, and came to Samuel unto Ramah, And said unto him, Behold, thou art old, and thy sons walk not in thy ways: now make us a king to judge us like all the nations. But the thing displeased Samuel, when they said, Give us a king to judge us. And Samuel prayed unto the Lord. And the Lord said unto Samuel, Hearken unto the voice of the people in all that they say unto thee: for they have not rejected thee, but they have rejected me, that I should not reign over them. According to all the works which they have done since the day that I brought them up out of Egypt even unto this day, wherewith they have forsaken me, and served other gods, so do they also unto thee. Now therefore hearken unto their voice: howbeit yet protest solemnly unto them, and shew them the manner of the king that shall reign over them. And Samuel told all the words of the Lord unto the people that asked of him a king. And he said, This will be the manner of the king that shall reign over you: He will take your sons, and appoint them for himself, for his chariots, and to be his horsemen; and some shall run before his chariots. And he will appoint him captains over thousands, and captains over fifties; and will set them to ear his ground, and to reap his harvest, and to make his instruments of war, and instruments of his chariots. And he will take your daughters to be confectioneries, and to be cooks, and to be bakers. And he will take your fields, and your vineyards, and your oliveyards, even the best of them, and give them to his servants. And he will take the tenth of your seed, and of your vineyards, and give to his officers, and to his servants. And he will take your menservants, and your maidservants, and your goodliest young men, and your asses, and put them to his work. He will take the tenth of your sheep: and ye shall be his servants. And ye shall cry out in that day because of your king which ye shall have chosen you; and the Lord will not hear you in that day. Nevertheless the people refused to obey the voice of Samuel; and they said, Nay; but we will have a king over us; That we also may be like all the nations; and that our king may judge us, and go out before us, and fight our battles. And Samuel heard all the words of the people, and he rehearsed them in the ears of the Lord. And the Lord said to Samuel, Hearken unto their voice, and make them a king. And Samuel said unto the men of Israel, Go ye every man unto his city."

God clearly did not want the people of Israel to have a king. In fact, He went to great lengths to explain through His prophet, Samuel, His will for them. But Israel, like many anointed Christian leaders today, dictated to God what they wanted for their personal lives and their nation.

The Lord clearly revealed to Israel His will and the cost that they and their children would have to pay to have a king. But Israel, because of an offense they received through Samuel's sons, did not give heed to His will.

It was this offense that blinded them to the Lord's leadership. However, God always honors faith, and He refuses to manipulate the free will of man. The Lord gave Israel their desire for a king!

Calling vs. Commissioning

Like many brethren in Christ throughout the ages, by the prophetic words spoken over my life in various meetings and through prayer and fasting, I was able to view from a distance God's purpose for my life. But driven by a fear produced by an overbalance of end-time teaching — that there would not be time to fulfill what God had purposed — I set out to fulfill my calling before the allotted time of my commissioning.

I had not allowed the Spirit of God to develop the abilities in my life by placing me alongside an experienced pastor in a local church, a man of God who could impart sound doctrine, regulate my growth, and enable my full abilities to develop so that I would not grow in a spiritually deformed manner, but be able to complete the race that had been set before me.

We have to allow the Spirit of God to do the necessary work that eventually brings about the true commissioning.

One of the great men recorded in the Bible who stepped out before his time was the apostle Paul. He was called on the road to Damascus, empowered a short time after, and immediately started to fulfill his call.

Paul found himself in all kinds of confrontations that eventually persuaded him to withdraw to a place of refuge, his hometown of Tarsus. After discerning what had happened to Paul, Barnabas ventured to Tarsus to rescue him from himself by becoming a role model or father-figure for him.

The Modern-Day Barnabas

I praise God for every Barnabas of today! I personally found one in the man whom I now call my pastor, Rev. Tommy Reid of the Full Gospel Tabernacle in Orchard Park, New York.

He is a man with the ability to see the potential in others without condemning them for where they are at. He is not intimidated by what they believe at that very moment in time, but in an authoritative manner, working in the Spirit like a master builder of souls, he has the ability to lead them to the place where God wants them to be.

I am sure Pastor Reid does not view himself in this manner. Bearing testimony to this fact, however, are numerous men and women who would not be in the ministry today if it were not for his heart of love, forgiveness, and acceptance.

Chapter 5

The Penalty for Disobedience

One of the greatest examples recorded in the Bible clearly revealing the path of destruction caused by one man's act of disobedience is found in the life of Jonathan, the son of King Saul.

As a young Christian, I heard many sermons preached on the great loyalty of Jonathan. This created a check in my spirit concerning God's faithfulness in rewarding every man according to his works of love. If Jonathan was such a great person, why did God give the throne to David, rather than the rightful heir, Prince Jonathan, the true son of Saul?

This question led me to study the Scriptures. I was led to a verse of Scripture that could not be shaken from my mind, and I realized that the Holy Spirit was attempting to reveal something to me. The Scripture I read was the conclusion of the confrontation that the prophet Samuel had with King Saul over the act of disobedience that cost Saul the throne.

The thing that amazed me was the fact that Saul, rather than taking the blame for his actions, blamed the people and made the following statement, "I have sinned, for I have transgressed the commandment of the Lord, and thy words, because I feared the people, and obeyed their voice."

It was this response of Saul's that prompted me to search the Scriptures to find out why he had attempted to shift the blame off himself onto the people.

 I became convinced that there had to be a specific time in Saul's life when he stopped being a vessel for God to reflect Himself through as the true King of Israel. It also became quite clear to me that Saul began to think more of his own opinions in certain situations than he did of the Lord's. These two facts are clearly evident when studying the outcome of the mission the Lord had given him to destroy the Amalekites.

Saul's order from above was to utterly destroy the Amalekites as well as their livestock. He did exactly this, except he brought back Agag, the king of the Amalekites, as a trophy for Israel, along with the best of the sheep and oxen to offer up as a sacrifice to the Lord.

This incident may seem harmless from a human viewpoint, but it was totally unacceptable to God. It was a personal act of rebellion against His leadership, and is why the prophet

Samuel made this proclamation to King Saul found in First Samuel 15:22,23, "And Samuel said, Hath the Lord as great delight in burnt offerings and sacrifices, as in obeying the voice of the Lord? Behold, to obey is better than sacrifice, and to hearken than the fat of rams. For rebellion is as the sin of witchcraft, and stubbornness is as iniquity and idolatry. Because thou hast rejected the word of the Lord, he hath also rejected thee from being king."

Friends, this exact situation happens in churches, businesses, and families. The person who has the responsibility of leadership will make a controversial decision only to be challenged by his partner.

The bystander cannot understand why the person who made the decision gets so upset over something that seems so trivial, not realizing that the person who was responsible for making the decision is having their position of authority challenged. *yes*

The line of authority must be drawn if there is to be genuine unity in business, family, or the church. There is an old saying that comes to mind: "Anything with more than one head is a monster, and anything without a head is a freak!"

Jonathan's Disobedience

I could not shake from my mind the original verse of Scripture the Lord gave me. I continually pondered, "Where did Saul listen to the people rather than God?" Anyone who knows the Lord realizes that He does not dismiss a person when a mistake is made. He always gives a space of time to repent and change before judgment. There had to be more to the severe judgment Saul received in this situation!

This question, revolving in my mind, led me to an event that happened between Saul and Jonathan. This event eventually cost Saul his throne and also disqualified Jonathan from inheriting it.

Seeds of Discontentment

Friends, I am going to take you to several events that are recorded in Scripture. These events are not recorded to expose Jonathan, but rather for our benefit so that we may learn by his mistakes.

Satan used the setting of wartime to plant the seeds of discontentment in Jonathan's life — a time when all ambitious young soldiers want to make a name for themselves; a time to prove their manhood to their older peers. This was Jonathan's perfect opportunity to show his father, the great King Saul, he was just as much a man as any of the great soldiers who served in the king's army.

Israel was at war with the Philistines and the battle was not going too well, prompting King

Saul to withdraw himself to seek counsel from the Lord. At this time Saul called a fast for all his soldiers. But Jonathan did not hear his father's command to stay put until they received the final clearance from God to proceed against the enemy. Scripture does not tell us why Jonathan did not hear the King's command. Maybe he really did hear, but chose the moment to prove himself!

In this instance, Jonathan can be likened to many Christians in the Body of Christ today. They think they have special privileges because their marriage partner, parent, sibling, or best friend has a genuine ministry, and they subconsciously believe that their personal relationship disqualifies them from the same standard of obedience governing the rest of the Body of Christ. Therefore, they presume they have the right to do whatever they think is right in their own eyes.

If only these Christians, along with Jonathan and Saul, had the wisdom of Solomon when he said, "There is a way that seems right to a man, but at the end thereof are the ways of death."

Sowing the Seeds of Discontentment

Jonathan then did something that was fatal to his destiny. He shared his discontentment with someone less mature and less experienced than himself. First Samuel 14:1 (NKJV) is where we pick up the record of this tragedy. "Now it happened one day that Jonathan the son of Saul said to the young man who bore his armour, 'Come, and let us go over to the Philistines' garrison that is on the other side.' But he did not tell his father."

Even though Jonathan went out to battle as part of the army, he took it upon himself to act independently of the God-given oversight of that army. The only person Jonathan took counsel with was his armorbearer.

true

Friends, when we need counsel, we should seek it from those more experienced than ourselves; those who can look at the problem through hindsight, which is perfect sight — not from our armorbearer, who is always someone less experienced than ourselves.

If, however, these people will not share their wisdom with you because of a fear of becoming involved, then go to the Word of God and ask the Holy Spirit to give you wisdom. He can guide you to numerous recorded events that will give you clear revelation.

Your peers, those who are your equal, or even your students will tell you what you want to hear to gain your acceptance, and will then discredit you when you blow yourself up!

No Lone Rangers in the Body of Christ

The following verses reveal that Jonathan never even told his fellow soldiers of his plans.

First Samuel 14:2,3 (NKJV), "And Saul was sitting in the outskirts of Gibeah under a pomegranate tree which is in Migron. The people who were with him were about six hundred men. Ahijah the son of Ahitub, Ichabod's brother, the son of Phinehas, the son of Eli, the Lord's priest in Shiloh, was wearing an ephod. But the people did not know that Jonathan had gone."

Brethren, it is essential to realize that God has placed us in a body of believers, and that we are dependent on one another. When we act alone, independent of the rest of the body, we endanger the whole body.

Paul explains this in First Corinthians 12:12-27, "For as the body is one, and hath many members, and all the members of that one body, being many, are one body: so also is Christ. For by one Spirit are we all baptized into one body, whether we be Jews or Gentiles, whether we be bond or free; and have been all made to drink into one Spirit. For the body is not one member, but many. If the foot shall say, Because I am not the hand, I am not of the body; is it therefore not of the body? And if the ear shall say, Because I am not the eye, I am not of the body; is it therefore not of the body? If the whole body were an eye, where were the hearing? If the whole were hearing, where were the smelling? But now hath God set the members every one of them in the body, as it hath pleased him. And if they were all one member, where were the body? But now are they many members, yet but one body. And the eye cannot say unto the hand, I have no need of thee: nor again the head to the feet, I have no need of you. Nay, much more those members of the body, which seem to be more feeble, are necessary: And those members of the body, which we think to be less honourable, upon these we bestow more abundant honour; and our uncomely parts have more abundant comeliness. For our comely parts have no need: but God hath tempered the body together, having given more abundant honour to that part which lacked: That there should be no schism in the body; but that the members should have the same care one for another. And whether one member suffer, all the members suffer with it; or one member be honoured, all the members rejoice with it. Now ye are the body of Christ, and members in particular."

It is extremely important that we do not break the unity of the Body of Christ through independent actions.

Let's pick up the record of these events in verses 16 and 17, where Jonathan was getting the victory over the Philistines.

"Now the watchmen of Saul in Gibeah of Benjamin looked, and there was the multitude, melting away; and they went here and there. Then Saul said to the people who were with him, 'Now call the roll and see who has gone from us.' And when they had called the roll, surprisingly, Jonathan and his armorbearer were not there."

Clearly, Jonathan acted independently of the army of Israel!

Accountability for Actions

The preceding verses reveal that at this point in Saul's life, he was still trying to fulfill the commission that God bestowed on him with integrity.

Immediately Saul realized that Jonathan and his armorbearer were missing, he sought counsel with the priest to find the will of God in this matter. But I personally believe that fear for his son's safety propelled Saul into battle before he heard from the Lord.

First Samuel 14:18-23 (NKJV), "And Saul said to Ahijah, 'Bring the ark of God here.' (for at that time the ark of God was with the children of Israel). Now it happened, while Saul talked to the priest, that the noise which was in the camp of the Philistines continued to increase; so Saul said to the priest, 'Withdraw your hand.' Then Saul and all the people who were with him assembled, and they went to the battle; and indeed every man's sword was against his neighbor, and there was very great confusion. Moreover the Hebrews who were with the Philistines before that time, who went up with them into the camp from the surrounding country, they also joined the Israelites who were with Saul and Jonathan. Likewise all the men of Israel who had hidden in the mountains of Ephraim, when they heard that the Philistines fled, they also followed hard after them in the battle. So the Lord saved Israel that day, and the battle shifted to Beth Aven."

Acts of Faith are Accountable

At this point I would like to make a statement that may rattle some folk; then again, it may set some free: The Lord will always honor genuine faith, but He will always bring acts of faith into accountability!

I personally believe this is what Jesus is referring to in Matthew 7:21-23 when He declared, "Not every one that saith unto me, Lord, Lord, shall enter into the kingdom of heaven; but he that doeth the will of my Father which is in heaven. Many will say to me in that day, Lord, Lord, have we not prophesied in thy name? and in thy name have cast out devils? and in thy name done many wonderful works? And then will I profess unto them, I never knew you: depart from me, ye that work iniquity."

The emphasis here is on the word, "iniquity." There are two words translated for sin in the Bible. One is transgression. The other is iniquity.

Transgression occurs when we are not sure whether or not something we have no clear revelation on is right to do. Iniquity occurs when we have clear instruction on the matter but still feel our own way is right. This is rebellion!

The Bible clearly states that the love of Christ will cover a multitude of transgressions, but an act of rebellion will always be brought into accountability. As we read on, we find that Jonathan learned this truth concerning God's nature.

Rebellion in the Camp

So let's again pick up the record in verses 24-32, where the devil uses Jonathan's new-found fame and popularity against Saul and God by provoking the army to rebel against Saul's leadership and the Mosaic law.

"And the men of Israel were distressed that day, for Saul had placed the people under oath, saying, 'Cursed is the man who eats any food until evening, before I have taken vengeance on my enemies.' So none of the people tasted food. Now all the people of the land came to a forest:

and there was honey on the ground. And when the people had come into the woods, there was the honey, dripping; but no one put his hand to his mouth, for the people feared the oath. But Jonathan had not heard his father charge the people with the oath; therefore he stretched out the end of the rod that was in his hand and dipped it in a honeycomb, and put his hand to his mouth; and his countenance brightened. Then one of the people said, 'Your father strictly charged the people with an oath, saying, Cursed is the man who eats food this day.' And the people were faint. But Jonathan said, 'My father has troubled the land, Look now, how my countenance has brightened because I tasted a little of this honey. How much better if the people had eaten freely today of the spoil of their enemies which they found! For now would there not have been a much greater slaughter among the Philistines?' Now they had driven back the Philistines that day from Michmash to Aijalon. So the people were very faint. And the people rushed on the spoil, and took sheep, oxen, and calves, and slaughtered them on the ground; and the people ate them with the blood."

true

The devil always takes advantage of an explosive situation! The discontentment the people felt for Saul because their bellies were empty, and the newly found fame that Jonathan was experiencing, created just the right atmosphere to get the people to sin against their God. For the devil to accomplish this, he first had to belittle King Saul in the sight of his army, and what better person to use than Saul's own son!

I personally believe this was accomplished when Jonathan learned a fast was called among the people. Knowing his father's character, Jonathan knew his father would share the credit of the victory with the whole army, placing an emphasis on the corporate fast of the people. This upset Jonathan!

Many modern-day preachers can again be likened to Jonathan in this instance. They truly believe that they are God's man of power for their city, and when another preacher moves into the area, they become threatened and make light of any triumphs this new ministry might be experiencing.

The emphasis is taken off other's victories so that they may be king for the day. They do not realize that God will eventually bring their actions into judgment.

Jonathan did just this by exposing his father. Whether King Saul was right or wrong, Jonathan's actions removed the restraints from the nation of Israel and caused the people to sin by consuming the animals with the blood.

God's Ways Are Not Our Ways

In the following verses, 33-35, we see that Saul tried desperately to correct the sin by bringing order back into the people.

"Then they told Saul, saying, 'Look, the people are sinning against the Lord by eating with the blood!' And he said, 'You have dealt treacherously: roll a large stone to me this day.' And Saul said, 'Disperse yourselves among the people, and say to them, "Bring me here every man's ox and every man's sheep, slaughter them here, and eat; and do not sin against the Lord by eating with the blood." So every one of the people brought his ox with him that night, and slaughtered it there. Then Saul built an altar to the Lord. This was the first altar that he built to the Lord."

Saul built an altar in his attempt to correct the wrong that had already been committed by Israel when they ate the flesh of the animals with the blood still in it.

However, his attempt to rectify the situation was futile, as we will see in the following verses, 36-44, "And Saul said, 'Let us go down after the Philistines by night, and plunder them until the morning light; and let us not leave a man of them.' And they said, 'Do whatever seems good to you.' Then the priest said, 'Let us draw near to God here.' So Saul asked counsel of God, 'Shall I go down after the Philistines? Will You deliver them into the hand of Israel?' But He did not answer him that day. And Saul said, 'Come over here, all you chiefs of the people, and know and see what this sin was today. For as the Lord lives, who saves Israel, though it be in Jonathan my son, he shall surely die.' But not a man among all the people answered him. Then he said to all Israel, 'You be on one side, and my son Jonathan and I will be on the other side.' And the people said to Saul, 'Do what seems good to you.' Therefore Saul said to the Lord God of Israel, 'Give a perfect lot.' So Saul and Jonathan were taken, but the people escaped. And Saul said, 'Cast lots between my son Jonathan and me.' So Jonathan was taken. Then Saul said to Jonathan, 'Tell me what you have done.' And Jonathan told him, and said, 'I only tasted a little honey with the end of the rod that was in my hand. So now I must die!' And Saul answered, 'God do so and more also; for you shall surely die, Jonathan.'"

It is very clear by these Scripture verses that Saul realized by now that even though he and the people believed that a great victory was won that day by the hand of Jonathan, the Lord did not view the matter in the same light, and He was demanding Saul to bring his son to accountability.

The following verses clearly define where Saul first feared the people, and gave in to their demands. Verses 45,46, "But the people said to Saul, 'Shall Jonathan die, who has accomplished this great salvation in Israel? Certainly not! As the Lord lives, not one hair of his head shall fall to the ground, for he has worked with God this day.' So the people rescued Jonathan, and he did not die. Then Saul returned from pursuing the Philistines, and the Philistines went to their own place."

Jonathan could have been saved that day without turning God against Saul. Saul and the people of Israel could have called out to God and interceded on behalf of Jonathan's immaturity!

Being the merciful God that He is, He would have spoken to the prophet Samuel and said, "I have heard the cries of Saul and the people of Israel for Jonathan and I have spared him this day."

The whole situation would have been made right in the sight of God. As it happened, it wasn't, because from that day King Saul started mingling his opinions with God's commands. This, and this alone, cost him the kingdom!

The Devil Did It!

Many Christians get into the extremity of spiritual warfare in the hope of making it further in the race of life by blaming every failure on the devil.

God will be faithful(

If their marriage partner resists them in their life's ventures, it's the devil. If the car breaks down, it's the devil. If they get sick, it's the devil. If financial pressure surmounts because of mismanagement, it's the devil. If their colleagues at work irritate them, it's the devil. If it rains the day they choose to go to the beach, it's the devil. If they loose their temper, it's the devil. If they commit adultery, it's the devil. If the pastor doesn't promote them when they believe he ought to, he's the devil!

The Devil is Not Ever Present

Satan has created a delusion in many Christians' minds that he is omnipresent. They believe that he is the same as God and can be everywhere at one time, or ever present.

Friends, the devil does not even know the names of most Christians, let alone what they do! In Acts 19:13-15, we find the record of a confrontation between the seven sons of Sceva and some demons.

"Then certain of the vagabond Jews, exorcists, took upon them to call over them which had evil spirits the name of the Lord Jesus, saying, We adjure you by Jesus whom Paul preacheth. And there were seven sons of one Sceva, a Jew, and chief of the priests, which did so. And the evil spirit answered and said, Jesus I know, and Paul I know; but who are ye?"

The original Greek accurately says, "Jesus I know, and Paul I'm getting to know." The Amplified version of the Bible records the verse in this manner. "But one evil spirit retorted, Jesus I know, and Paul I know about, but who are you?"

It is about time Christians stopped blaming the devil for their failures. Furthermore, in order to justify our own failures, we have to stop casting the shadow of failure over the mighty men and women of the Bible. Yes, these mighty men and women were attacked, but they did win every fight they fought, both natural and spiritual. These men and women were only defeated when they walked in disobedience.

Submit Yourself to God

The greatest weapon that the Church has against the devil is submission. James makes this clear when he says, "Submit yourselves to God, resist the devil, and he will flee from you." How do we resist the devil? Clearly by submitting to God!

You can shout at the devil until you are "blue in the face." You can fast until you are so skinny that you have to run around in the shower to get wet. But the Bible will still say, "Humble yourself under the mighty hand of God, that in due time He may exalt you."

Have you ever considered that the hand of God is the apostles, prophets, evangelists, pastors, and teachers — the five fingers of God's hand that shapes the believer's life, changing him from boyhood to manhood?

Chapter 6
Walking Out of Failure

The first thing that must be done in order to walk out of failure is to change the direction you've been heading. Frankly, to continue doing the same things over and over again and expect different results is a form of insanity. Yet so many people do just this!

The first question you must ask yourself is, "What do I want out of this life that Jesus Christ purchased for me on Calvary?" If your response is more money, a better job, a happy marriage, a nice home, to lose weight, a new vehicle, or to be accepted in the ministry, then your problem is right there!

Solomon, at the conclusion of writing the book of Ecclesiastes, made this statement in chapter 12:13,14, "Let us hear the conclusion of the whole matter: Fear God, and keep his commandments: for this is the whole duty of man. For God shall bring every work into judgment, with every secret thing, whether it be good, or whether it be evil."

The Lord Jesus reinforces Solomon's statement. In Matthew 6:19-34, the key to the sermon that He preached on that day is clearly found in verse 33, where He says, "But seek ye first the kingdom of God, and his righteousness; and all these things shall be added unto you."

The Kingdom of God and the Kingdom of Heaven

Many Christians are confused between the kingdom of God and the kingdom of Heaven. One kingdom is a tangible place; the other kingdom is the actual rule of God in the believer's life.

You will still get to Heaven if you have anxiety in your life, as getting to Heaven does not depend on your works. You can live a defeated life in many areas of your Christian life and still get to Heaven by releasing faith in the blood of Jesus for the forgiveness of sin.

Put simply, you can be saved from the eternal fire of hell but still battle sickness, poverty, a bad marriage, broken relationships, and various addictions in this life. But you will never have the absolute rule of God in your life on this earth while the flesh dominates the spirit.

Galatians 5:16-21 confirms this. "This I say then, Walk in the Spirit and ye shall not fulfill the lust of the flesh. For the flesh lusteth against the Spirit, and the Spirit against the flesh: and these are contrary the one to the other: so that ye cannot do the things that ye would. But if ye be led of the Spirit, ye are not under the law. Now the works of the flesh are manifest, which are these; Adultery, fornication, uncleanness, lasciviousness, idolatry, witchcraft, hatred, variance, emulations, wrath, strife, seditions, heresies, envyings, murders, drunkenness, revellings, and such like: of the which I tell you before, as I have also told you in time past, that they which do such things shall not inherit the kingdom of God."

The apostle Paul said the kingdom of God shall not be inherited by those who do these things. He did not say that you would not inherit the kingdom of Heaven.

If Paul had made this statement he would have contradicted himself, as he also said in Galatians 2:16, "Knowing that a man is not justified by the works of the law, but by the faith of Jesus Christ, even we have believed in Jesus Christ, that we might be justified by the faith of Christ, and not by the works of the law: for by the works of the law shall no flesh be justified."

Paul repeats himself in verse 21 by saying, "I do not frustrate the grace of God: for if righteousness come by the law, then Christ is dead in vain." Paul again declares in Ephesians 2:8-9, "For by grace are ye saved through faith; and that not of yourselves: it is the gift of God: Not of works, lest any man should boast."

Friends, if you can make the simple adjustment in your doctrinal stand to see the kingdom of God and the kingdom of Heaven as two different kingdoms, the message to the saved and the unsaved makes a lot more sense.

His Acceptance Through His Love

The preceding Scriptures clearly tell us that our works do not obtain God's love or His acceptance of us. We already have His acceptance through His love that we know passes all understanding.

We must come to the revelation that even though we might lead 10,000 people to Christ, birth 1,000 churches, bathe and clean our teeth five times a day, change our clothes ten times a day, give up smoking, drinking, and drugs, or even memorize the Bible from Genesis to Revelation, we could not be any more loved than the first moment we accepted Jesus as our Savior.

As a matter of fact, God loved us long before we accepted Christ as Savior. The Bible declares that while we were still sinners, He loved us and gave His Son to die on the cross for us!

However, the respect of the Lord is obtained by our obedience to Him. The Word declares that if we are found faithful in the little things that He asks us to do, He will entrust us with greater things. The giftings of God are not given through emotional favoritism, but rather through the development of our ability through faithfulness.

Possessions or Riches?

The simple truth is that gain is not godliness. Many Christians feel they have not accomplished anything in God unless they have a new Cadillac, a five-bedroom house with an ocean view, the most expensive clothes and cologne money can buy, and eat at the finest restaurants.

Material riches are not evil. They can be achieved through a worshipful relationship with Jesus Christ. However, they are not the evidence of a worshipful relationship with Christ.

Many worldly people have achieved the success and riches of this world, such as Elvis Presley, Jimi Hendrix, Janis Joplin, as well as many thousands of others who have killed themselves by drug overdoses in their search for genuine peace.

There is nothing wrong with having money or the finer things of this life. It is the love of material possessions that corrupts! This was the problem with the rich young ruler who came to Jesus seeking eternal life. The Bible declares that this man had many possessions. The difference between possessions and riches is simply this: Possessions control you; you control riches!

I truly believe that Agur understood this principle when he wrote in Proverbs 30:7-9,

"Two things that I required of thee; deny me them not before I die: Remove far from me vanity and lies: give me neither poverty nor riches; feed me with food convenient for me: Lest I be full, and deny thee, and say, Who is the Lord? or lest I be poor, and steal, and take the name of my God in vain."

Does God have Schizophrenia?

I have been told of a survey completed recently by a group of sociologists who had determined amongst themselves to find out what Christians really believed concerning the devil and God. The team asked one thousand Christians a series of questions concerning the nature of God and the nature of the devil. This information was then fed into a computer.

Much to their surprise, the results revealed that Christians actually believed that the devil is the dark side of God's nature!

The same God who healed was the same God who made them sick. The same God who gave prosperity was the same God who gave poverty. The same God who gave life was the same God who took life. As a matter of fact, the sociologists claimed that the computer diagnosed God to have the perfect nature of a schizophrenic.

Get the Gospel Straight

It is a terrible shame that so many Christians speak with such conviction on subjects that they have no real understanding of.

I have sat in church meetings and have heard the preacher begin his message by telling the congregation that Jesus Christ totally defeated the devil on the cross of Calvary and set the captives free.

By the conclusion of the message, the preacher is convincing the listeners that the Lord botched the job and now it is up to the Church to deal with the devil all over again.

No wonder so many sincere Christians are confused. Friends, let's get the gospel straight and stick to it!

The Right Motivation

In conclusion, I cannot stress enough that most failures enter our lives because of wrong motivation. The entire reason that we live and breathe and have our being is to do the will of God. And if this means serving Him in Africa, India, or middle America, let's not do it for self-gain, but for the extension of His kingdom here upon the earth.

Chapter 7
Making a Quality Decision

There is an old saying, "The road to Someday leads to a town called Nowhere." Procrastation within the believer's life is a stronghold that has to be dealt with.

Once we are saved and filled with the Holy Ghost, we are empowered to achieve great things by the greater One that is within us. But many believers bring into their Christian lives many fears — fears such as: the fear of man, the fear of failure, the fear of pain, the fear of rejection, the fear of the unknown, or even the fear of success.

These fears hinder many believers from making a quality decision to do what God requires and so stops them from achieving all that He has purposed for their lives.

James informs that a double minded man is unstable in all his ways and that he should expect nothing from the Lord. It is double mindedness that causes the believer to procrastinate, wavering between two opinions. Procrastination will eventually lead to a sense of failure and cause the believer to become lethargic in his everyday life.

Confront Your Fears

It seems for some believers there is no easy deliverance from the fears that dominate. They go from altar call to altar call seeking freedom by the laying on of hands or by a few magic words from some preacher. Sadly, years pass and their fears still remain evident in their lives.

The only way to overcome fear is to make a quality decision to confront it! When the decision to confront the fear is made, the Holy Spirit will come upon the believer to empower him to follow through with his decision.

Set Free!

I would like to share how I personally overcame my greatest fears. In the world system, I was known by my peers as a fearless person. They had witnessed me engineer some of the most daring robberies in our country and not even raise a sweat. They had seen me shot at and knifed — only to joke about it a few minutes later.

But after I received Christ as my Savior, various fears surfaced from within my soul. The greatest of these was the fear of public speaking.

This fear manifested itself every Sunday morning when I would go to church.

Our pastor was a preacher who would, at random, ask several people to testify or open or close in prayer. I would sit in the congregation with a great knot in my stomach that literally made me sick, fearing I would be asked to testify or pray.

Eventually, one Sunday morning the pastor asked my brother-in-law to open in prayer. This "freaked me out"! It was just too close for comfort. So after the meeting, when the pastor went out to his prayer room, I followed him. I politely informed him that if he ever asked me to pray or testify publicly, I would walk right out to the front of the church and knock him out. He assured me that he would never ask me.

The following Sunday morning was the first Sunday that I felt comfortable about going to church. Gerri and I had no sooner walked into the church and sat down, when the pastor asked me to open the service in prayer. He was struck dumb! It was obvious he had asked me before he realized what he was doing. He stared at me, waiting for my reaction.

Well, the next thirty seconds seemed like thirty minutes as I decided what to do. It seemed like every person in the congregation was staring right at me.

I stood to my feet. As I did, an electrical current rushed through my being. I opened my mouth to speak, and the words came out with an incredible flow that startled me.

Even after this powerful experience, I was still terrified to speak in public. But whenever I made the decision to confront the fear and speak, it became easier.

Finally, one night, the fear completely broke when I was asked to give my testimony at a church in the Australian country town of Lismore. As I proceeded down the aisle to the pulpit to speak, I was having dizzy spells from the fear I was suffering. On the way toward the pulpit someone laid their hand on my shoulder and said, "Tell them how much you love Me!"

I turned to see who spoke to me. No one was near me, but I could still feel His Hand on my shoulder. At that moment, great boldness came over me, and I have never had a problem with speaking publicly since that day.

The release the Lord gave me that night could never have happened if, initially, I did not make the decision to overcome this fear by confronting it.

A Fool For Christ

The next fear I had to overcome was the fear of rejection. The fear of rejection would manifest itself whenever I tried to witness to a stranger.

I remember the first time I decided to confront this fear. That morning I got all prayed up in the Spirit and drove to the local mall. Our pastor had given me several different types of tracts to hand out. I must have walked through that mall at least ten times before I worked up the courage to speak to someone.

The person I chose was an elderly lady. I was so sure she would be gentle with me. So I approached her and asked if I could share Jesus with her. She began to scream at me and I ran back to my car shaking.

I must have sat there for thirty minutes before I could even drive the vehicle. As I headed home, I made the decision that this was definitely not my ministry.

On arriving home, I shared with Gerri what had happened. She simply replied that if I was going to be a minister of the gospel I would have to go back and try again.

Isn't it amazing how we have all this wonderful advice for others but never take our own advice? However, I took her advice and immediately went back out to witness to overcome my fear.

As I was driving, I noticed an elderly man who I knew. I thought to myself, "This looks like a good opportunity." So I stopped my vehicle, approached him, and began to tell him the gospel story.

Believe it or not, he also began to shout at me and said, "Don't tell me about God. Where was God when my friends were getting killed in the Second World War?"

I left him totally broken. As a matter of fact, he left me with more questions in my mind than I'm sure I left in his.

I determined never to do this type of ministry again. But this decision only left a sense of failure in my life, as I truly believed that God had called me at that time to do the work of an evangelist.

This now seemed impossible! Even though I had conquered my fear of public speaking in the church where I felt safe, I still could not approach the sinner in the street. I reminded myself of a small dog that was real brave in his own front yard when he was confronted by a larger dog passing by. But if he met this dog down the road, he would surely run home to hide.

This sense of failure lasted for several weeks. Every day, defeat ran around inside my head like a freight train, until one day I was out doing the grocery shopping with Gerri at a large supermarket. She was pushing the shopping cart and I was loading the groceries into the cart.

An audible voice spoke to me and with sarcasm said, "You be an evangelist? Give it up now, and go back to work before you make a complete fool of yourself!"

I should have realized that the devil was a liar, because I had already made a complete fool of myself. But this is not what happened. Hot flushes ran through my body.

He continued, "If you are truly an evangelist, there are a lot of people here who need to be saved. Tell them about your Jesus!"

I looked up, and we were now just by the check-out. There were people everywhere. For a moment I stood there, motionless with fear. At this crucial moment, I made the decision to overcome and not be overcome!

The words bellowed out of my mouth, "In the Name of Jesus, I want to tell you all of the saving grace of the Lord Jesus Christ." As the words rushed from my mouth, the same electricity flowed through my body that I had experienced the first time my pastor asked me to open in prayer. Through the corner of my eye, I saw Gerri scurrying down the aisle with the shopping cart, leaving me all alone.

A man in a wheelchair cruised around the corner to see what all the commotion was. I yelled at him, "God can raise you out of that chair that holds you a prisoner." Friends, he maneuvered that wheelchair and dashed off, with me after him. Thank God I never caught him!

But, praise God, that the quality decision I made that day, set me free from the fear of rejection. I have since led people to the Lord all over the world in taxi cabs, train stations, airports, on planes, in restaurants, at shopping malls, and many other places too numerous to mention.

A Quality Decision

You see friends, the devil knows when you are not convinced in your own mind. He knows when you say you will do something with your whole heart, half your heart, or a quarter of your heart. It is only when you make that quality decision that the devil knows he has no more authority over you.

So a quality decision is one of the most important ingredients that must be applied to walk out of the emotional strain of failure. Frankly, we really do not enter into failure until we have given up. A setback in life's experiences is only classified as a failure when we give up and refuse to go any further.

A perfect example can be taken from the life of the rock and roll singer, Jerry Lee Lewis. At the peak of his singing career he experienced a setback when he married an under-aged girl. His actions were rejected by his fans and the moral majority of America. Newspaper and television headlines around the world broadcasted his fall from fame. It was only the tenacity that burned within his soul that caused him to fight his way back to popularity. In time, his success drowned out the screams of his fall.

I pray to God that his cousin, Jimmy Swaggart, has the same intestinal fortitude to fight back against impossible odds. Please don't misunderstand me. I am not condoning either of these men's actions that brought about their fall. But as an observer, I cannot help but admire Jerry Lee's stand to fight back and win under such incredible odds.

If a person from the world system can accomplish such a great feat, surely Christians governed by a better system than the world; that is, the principles of love, forgiveness, and acceptance, can do the same.

Knocked Down, But Not Knocked Out!

There is a greater sin than the sin that causes a person to fall from grace and that is the sin to continue to live in the self-pity produced by the shame and guilt of the fall from grace. There has to come a time in a person's life when he makes the decision to get up off the floor and fight back.

There is a verse of Scripture in Phillips' translation of the New Testament where the apostle Paul declares, "I am knocked down, but I am not knocked out."

This Scripture has ministered to me over the years. As an ex-boxer, I can relate to Paul's statement. When I fought in the boxing ring there were times when I did not want to get up off the mat, consoling myself, "Why should I get up? He will only knock me down again." But you have to get up!

The principle of being "knocked down, but not knocked out" applies to all the issues of life — whether it be in marriage, in business, in friendship, in a financial investment, in a pastorate, or simply in poor grades at school. You are only defeated when you refuse to stand up and fight for what you really want to accomplish in this life!

Just because you experience a few setbacks does not mean the end of the world has come. If this were true, Lee Iacocca, the president of Chrysler Corporation, didn't know anything about it! If it were not for a failure in his life, when he was fired from the Ford Motor Company, he never would have bought into Chrysler and become the celebrated success he is today.

The same can be said for Thomas Watson. He started the world-renowned company, IBM, because he was fired from a similar company. He bounced back from his failure to dwarf the company from which he was fired. Friends, there is an old saying, "It is not the size of the dog in the fight, it is the size of the fight in the dog!"

Set Before You is Life or Death

One of the most notable times recorded in the Bible concerning the Israelites having to make a quality decision is when Moses brought them back to the exact place where their forefathers had rebelled against God forty years before.

Moses charged them that they should obey God and enter into the promised land. This is recorded in Deuteronomy 30:19,20, "I call heaven and earth to record this day against you, that I have set before you life and death, blessing and cursing: therefore choose life, that both thou and thy seed may live: That thou mayest love the Lord thy God, and that thou mayest obey his voice, and that thou mayest cleave unto him: for he is thy life, and the length of thy days: that thou mayest dwell in the land which the Lord sware unto thy fathers, to Abraham, to Isaac, and to Jacob, to give them."

Praise God! History bears witness that the people of Israel did make the right decision, and entered into the promised land. And the Lord God did remain faithful to His Word by delivering it unto them.

He will do the same for all His children, if we will lean not to our own understanding and acknowledge Him in all our ways.

Chapter 8

Establishing Role Models

Whether we want to admit it or not, we all learn from somebody. Jesus said that a man can never be greater than his teacher. In making this statement, the Lord was clearly revealing that we need to be taught.

Man was not pre-programmed at birth, as some would have you believe. Others teach that we do not need any man to instruct us, because the Holy Spirit will teach us all the things that pertain to the nature of God. The foundation for this doctrine is generally backed up with the following Scriptures:

First John 2:27, "But the anointing which ye have received of him abideth in you, and ye need not that any man teach you: but as the same anointing teacheth you of all things, and is truth, and is no lie, and even as it hath taught you, ye shall abide in him."

First Corinthians 2:13, "Which things also we speak, not in the words which man's wis-

dom teacheth, but which the Holy Ghost teacheth; comparing spiritual things with spiritual."

John 14:26, "But the Comforter, which is the
Holy Ghost, whom the Father will send in my
name, he shall teach you all things, and bring all
things to your remembrance, whatsoever I have
said unto you."

The thing that really amazes me is simply
this: if these people really do believe this doctrine that they preach, what in the world are
they doing trying to teach people?

When you read the preceding Scriptures by
themselves, this doctrine seems quite genuine.
But we must never forget that Scripture inter-
prets Scripture; for example, when these Scriptures are coupled with Ephesians 4:11-14, where
Paul said:

"And he gave some, apostles; and some,
prophets; and some, evangelists; and some, pastors and teachers; For the perfecting of the saints,
for the work of the ministry, for the edifying of
the body of Christ: Till we all come in the unity
of the faith, and of the knowledge of the Son of
God, unto a perfect man, unto the measure of
the stature of the fullness of Christ: That we
henceforth be no more children, tossed to and
fro, and carried about with every wind of doctrine, by the sleight of men, and cunning craftiness, whereby they lie in wait to deceive."

Either the Holy Spirit was confused when He gave Ephesians 4:11-14, or these verses need the other verses to exist. I personally believe that they need one another to exist — just as the Word was with God and the Word was God.

The Ultimate Role Model

The Word had to become flesh by taking on the form of humanity. This had to happen to allow God to come and dwell among mankind to be the ultimate role model for man, giving him a standard to obtain.

The Word of God now becomes flesh in the five-fold ministry gifts that He has placed in the body — His Church. Why? To perfect the saints, or more simply said, to teach the saints to bring them into the work of the ministry.

We see this demonstrated by the apostle Paul where he instructs Timothy in Second Timothy 2:2 *(Amplified)*, "And the (instructions) which you have heard from me, along with many witnesses, transmit and entrust (as a deposit) to reliable and faithful men who will be competent and qualified to teach others also."

We can also find in other places of the Word of God where the gifting that the Lord entrusted to a particular man taught other men. For example, Elisha learned from Elijah, Paul learned from Barnabas, Timothy learned from Paul, the twelve disciples learned from

Jesus, and Apollos learned from Aquila and Priscilla. Even though it was man instructing man, it was the wisdom of the Holy Spirit in their lives that taught these people.

Make the Right Choice

Most people suffer failure because they have established the wrong role models in their lives. It is not that these people do not have the ability to succeed. Everyone needs a good trainer to bring out the best in them, to cause them to rise to their fullest potential.

The life of the boxing champion, Mike Tyson, is a good example. When he first began his boxing career, Tyson had a trainer who truly loved him and desired to see him rise to his fullest potential. Tyson excelled to the point of becoming the youngest world heavyweight champion on record.

Then he changed trainers, or role models. It was only a matter of time before the decline in his performance as a boxer, and a person in general, was witnessed by the world.

What happened? Did Tyson lose his potential? No, he switched role models. His new role model brought out the worst in him, rather than the best. Tyson did not have to be a prophet or a spiritualist to discern the motivation of his new trainer and promoter.

For Tyson to now recover from his setback, he needs to face up to the fact that he cannot blame anyone else for his failures. He has to stand in front of the mirror, point at the first person he sees, and say, "You're to blame!"

James makes this quite plain when he says that a man is led astray by the lust in his own heart. We have to stop blaming others for our failures, and realize that God has given us a will.

The Will of Man

We can use our wills like Satan did when he said, "I will ascend into heaven. I will exalt my throne above the stars of God. I will sit also on the mount of the congregation, in the sides of the north. I will ascend above the heights of the clouds. I will be like the Most High." Or, we can use our will like the great King David when he said, "I will bless the Lord at all times, His praise shall always be in my mouth. I will keep my mouth with a bridle."

In Psalm 77 and Psalm 78 we find the six "I wills" of David where he says, "I will remember the years of the right hand of the most High. I will remember the works of the Lord. I will remember thy wonders of old. I will meditate also of all thy work, and talk of thy doings. I will open my mouth in a parable. I will utter dark sayings of old."

Friends, all too often I have heard people make these statements, "I didn't mean to hurt you!" "I just fell into adultery!" "I didn't mean to become a drunk!" "I didn't mean to get hooked on heroin!" "I didn't mean to tell a lie!"

These statements may be genuine in their minds, but unless we learn to use the greatest possession that God has given to mankind — the will — we will always make excuses for our failures.

It is about time we used our wills to love, used our wills to stay faithful, used our wills to study, used our wills to stay sober, used our wills to be a good partner in marriage, used our wills to be a good parent, and used our wills to diet to lose weight.

The Road Is Already Paved

After experiencing the crisis with the church in Australia in the early stages of my ministry, I decided to use my will to become the best that I possibly could be for God. I was motivated by a verse of Scripture that God gave me from the book of Proverbs which says (paraphrased), "If you walk with wise men you will become wise. If you walk with foolish men you will become foolish."

I decided not to "reinvent the wheel," but to develop relationships with people who I considered to be good role models, not dreamers: Men and women who had already "paved the way" of success in their own lives. People who know how to study. People who know how to present themselves. People who are successful in business. People who are successful in ministry. People who have good marriages. People who know how to handle the success and wealth they have obtained.

This was the very decision that changed my life and allowed me to accomplish the things that I have today. It does not matter how much potential you have or how capable your trainer is, unless you make the decision to submit your will to change!

I pray that this book has blessed and encouraged you. I would like to pray this prayer with you. It is a prayer that I prayed, allowing God to come into my life by His Spirit, to lead me out of the frustration of a sense of failure and set a straight path for my feet to follow.

"Dear Father, I have been wounded in the realm of my spirit man. I do not blame anyone else but myself for this hurt I have experienced.

"I ask You to forgive me for the times that I have been led astray by my own lusts. I ask You to come into my life by Your Spirit and go where no doctor's scalpel can go, right down into the depths of my being. Heal my broken and bruised spirit.

"Empower me again by Your Spirit to be strengthened in my inner man to complete the course that You have set before me. Just like Joshua of old, I make the decision: As from this day, my family and I will serve the Lord! Lead me to the men and women who can best teach me Your nature, and give me the ability to submit to them so that your purpose can truly be established in my life, in Jesus' Name. Amen."

Other books by Dr. Wayne C. Gwilliam:

The Potential of The Redeemed Mind
The Priest of A New Covenant
Back ot Basics
(21 Lesson Foundational Study Manual)

If this book, *Facing Up to Failure*, has ministered to you, and you would like a study program that ministers step-by-step principles of building a strong life in Christ, as found in Second Peter 1, please contact us as follows:

Reach Out School of Ministries
P.O. Box 2035
Hyde Park, NY 12538
(914) 229-6080